IELTS LISTENING STRATEGIES

The Ultimate Guide With Tips, Tricks, And Practice On How To Get A Target Band Score Of 8.0+ In 10 Minutes A Day

RACHEL MITCHELL

ISBN: 9781973361527

TABLE OF CONTENT

INTRODUCTION

Thank you and congratulate you for downloading the book *"IELTS Listening Strategies: The Ultimate Guide With Tips, Tricks, And Practice On How To Get A Target Band Score Of 8.0+ In 10 Minutes A Day."*

This book is well designed and written by an experienced native teacher from the USA who has been teaching IELTS for over 10 years. She really is the expert in training IELTS for students at each level. In this book, she will provide you all proven Formulas, Tips, Tricks, Strategies, Explanations, Structures, Listening Language, and Vocabulary to help you easily achieve an 8.0+ in the IELTS Listening, even if your listening is not excellent. This book will also walk you through step-by-step on how to develop your listening skill; clearly analyze and explain the different types of questions that are asked for the IELTS Listening Test; provide you step-by-step instructions on how to answer each type of question excellently.

As the author of this book, Rachel Mitchell believes that this book will be an indispensable reference and trusted guide for you who may want to maximize your band score in IELTS Listening. Once you read this book, I guarantee you that you will have learned an extraordinarily wide range of useful, and practical IELTS Listening strategies and formulas that will help you become a successful IELTS taker as well as you will even become a successful English user in work and in life within a short period of time only.

Take action today and start getting better scores tomorrow!

Thank you again for purchasing this book, and I hope you enjoy it.

IELTS LISTENING TEST
INTRODUCTION

- The Listening test is the **first module** of the IELTS test. All IELTS students take the same listening test. So, if you're taking academic IELTS or general training IELTS, you all take the same test, the same questions, the same format, and the same scoring.

- It takes approximately **30 minutes**, then candidates are given an extra **10 minutes at the end** to transfer their answers from their Question Booklet to their Answer Sheet.

- There are **4 sections** with **10 questions each** (40 questions). The first two sections are the easiest; they are social. That means the context of the situation is a social situation (an everyday situation) and the last two sections are more difficult, they are academic in content.

- The recording is heard only once. Ensure you listen carefully. If you miss something, there's no second chance. That means you really are multitasking during this listening test. You need to listen to the recording, read the questions and at the same time write down your answers. It can be quite difficult and it's something that you do need to practice.

- Test gets more difficult as it continues.

- There are a total of **40 questions**, with 10 questions per section. **A variety of tasks that may be presented** in the Listening test (e.g., Multiple Choice, Short Answer, Form Completion, sentence completion, labeling diagrams, etc...).

- Candidates are given time to read the questions before they listen and time to check their answers after they listen.
- Candidates must use a **pencil** to write answers on the Answer Sheet because it is scanned by a computer. That's the same as the IELTS reading test.

IELTS LISTENING FORMAT

Sections 1 & 2:

Everyday activities and common settings *(Shopping, registering for a course, renting an apartment, hotel and restaurant reservations, getting repairs, nature and animals, etc.)*

Section 1: the section 1 has **two speakers** (a social situation). A typical example is **a phone conversation** where somebody is **registering for a course**. For example, you want to book a course and they need to know what date; they need your name; they need your address, your telephone number. Or perhaps, you're **booking a table at a restaurant** or **organizing to meet someone** and you need to think of the time that you're going to meet. It's very specific information and it is quite easy to improve your score for this section. This section is the easiest of the four sections because you are asked to listen for basic information such as names, numbers, dates and locations.

Here is a sample Section 1 from a Question Booklet.

Questions 1-5

Write **NO MORE THAN ONE WORD**

VIDEO LIBRARY APPLICATION FORM

EXAMPLE   *ANSWER*
Surname   Jones

First names: Louise Cynthia

Address: Apartment 1, 72 **(1)** .... Street Highbridge

Post code: **(2)** ....

Telephone: 9835 6712 (home)   **(3)** .... (work)

Driver's licence number: **(4)** ....

DOB: 25th Month: **(5)** .... Year: 1977

Questions 6—8

Write **THREE** *letters* **A-F**.

What types of films does Louise like?
A   Action
B   Comedies
C   Musicals
D   Romance
E   Westerns
F   Wildlife

Questions 9 and 10
Write **NO MORE THAN 3 WORDS** .

9. How much does it cost to join the library?
10. When will Louise's card be ready?

Section 2: the section 2 is also social (everyday situations) but there is **only one speaker**. A typical example would be **a tour guide**. It would be a tour guide explaining about a resort, for example, *what facilities there are* or *the history behind the resort.* Another example could be, for example, talking about **an historic building** or talking about **a charity, a company or an organization**.

Here is a sample Section 2 from a Question Booklet.

Expedition Across Attora Mountains

Leader: Charles Owen

Prepared a **(11)** .... for the trip

Total length of trip **(12)** ....

Climbed highest peak in **(13)** ....

14. What took the group by surprise?
    A the amount of rain
    B the number of possible routes
    C the length of the journey

15. How did Charles feel about having to change routes?
    A He reluctantly accepted it.
    B He was irritated by the diversion.
    C It made no difference to enjoyment.

What does Charles say about his friends?
A   He met them at one stage on the trip.
B   They kept all their meeting arrangements.
C   One of them helped arrange the transport.
D   One of them owned the hotel they stayed in.
E   Some of them travelled with him.
F   Only one group lasted the 96 days.

What does Charles say about the donkeys?
A   He rode them when he was tired
B   He named them after places.
C   One of them died.
D   They behaved unpredictably.
E   They were very small.

Sections 3 & 4:

Academic settings *(seminars, lectures, training, tutors and students discussing assignments, etc.)*

Section 3: the section 3 is academic (the first academic section) that has **three to four speakers**. This is challenging because it's a discussion **(an academic discussion)**. When you've got three to four speakers that means you've got **different voices** and you have to be able to identify who is speaking. That could be quite challenging, but the most difficult is the section four.

Here is a sample Section 3 from a Question Booklet.

SECTION 3

Questions 21-25
Write **NO MORE THAN THREE WORDS** for each answer.

	Tim	Jane
Day of arrival	Sunday	(21) ....
Subject	History	(22) ....
Number of books to read	(23)	(24) ....
Day of first lecture	Tuesday	(25) ....

Questions 26-30
Write **NO MORE THAN THREE WORDS** for each answer.

26. What is Jane's study strategy in lectures?
27. What's Tim's study strategy for reading?
28. What is the subject of Tim's first lecture?
29. What's the title of Tim's first essay?
30. What is the subject of Jane's first essay?

Section 4: there is **only one speaker** and it is an academic lecture (very often involves a university lecturer speaking on an academic topic). This section is the most difficult, because you are asked to listen to a longer lecture.

Here is a sample Section 4 from a Question Booklet.

Questions 31-35

Write **NO MORE THAN THREE WORDS** for each answer.

Course	Type of course: duration & level	Entry requirements
Physical Fitness Instructor	Example: Six-month certificate	None
Sports Administrator	(31)	(32) .... in sports administration
Sports Psychologist	(33)	Degree in psychology
Physical Education Teacher	4 years degree in education	(34) ....
Recreation officer	(35)	None

Questions 36-40

Write the appropriate letters **A-G** against question 36- 40

MAIN ROLES

Job	Main Role
Physical Fitness Instructor	(36)
Sports Administrator	(37)
Sports Psychologist	(38)
Physical Education Teacher	(39)
Recreation Officer	(40)

A the coaching of teams

B the support of elite athletes

C guidance of ordinary individuals

D community health

E the treatment of injuries

F arranging matches and venues

G the rounded development of children

IELTS LISTENING MARKING AND ASSESSMENT:

- The scores are calculated by the number of correct answers you have. There are **40 questions** which is equivalent to **40 points**. Each time you get a correct answer, you get a point. That is how your band scores are calculated.

- You have to **follow the Instructions exactly** (e.g. must stay within word/number limit).

- **Spelling and grammar must be correct** *(e.g. singular or plural; use the correct form of the words)*. You will lose marks if you misspell a word or if you put a word in the wrong grammatical form. Of course, when you're listening, you don't have time to think about spelling. However, at the end of your test, you have **10 minutes** to transfer your answers to the answer sheet. That is the time for you to pay attention to spelling. Pay attention to your spelling, capital letters, and check the grammar. Use the ten minutes for transferring answers wisely.

Here is a list of difficult words. Try to practice spelling them correctly.

1. quite and quiet

2. choose and choice

3. business

4. address

5. questionnaire

6. government

7. environment

8. career

9. necessary

- **The scores for band score five, six, seven and eight**

Band 5.5 = 20 – 22 correct answers.

Band 6.0 = 23 – 26 correct answers.

Band 6.5 = 27 – 29 correct answers.

Band 7.0 = 30 – 32 correct answers.

Band 7.5 = 33 – 34 correct answers.

Band 8.0 = 35 – 37 correct answers.

Band 8.5 = 38 – 39 correct answers.

IELTS LISTENING QUESTION TYPES:

These are the **4** most common question types in the IELTS Listening test:

1. MULTIPLE CHOICE QUESTIONS:

This type of question asks you to choose the correct answer or answers from a list of three or four choices.

Question 19
Choose **TWO** letters **A-E**.

Which **TWO** groups of patients receive free medication?
A   people over 17 years old
B   unemployed people
C   non-UK residents
D   people over 60 years old
E   pregnant women

Questions 21-24
Circle the correct answer.

21. At first Fiona thinks that Martin's tutorial topic is
   A. inappropriate.
   B. dull.
   C. interesting.
   D. fascinating.

22. According to Martin, the banana
   A. has only recently been cultivated.
   B. is economical to grow.
   C. is good for your health.
   D. is his favourite food.

Question 21-26

Which company website has the following features?

A Hills Cycles website
B Wheels Unlimited website
C both websites

Write the correct letter, A, B, or C next to questions **21–26**.

21. bicycle catalogue ....
22. price list ....
23. bicycle accessories ....
24. company history ....
25. online ordering ....
26. moving graphics ....

Question 38-40

What does the lecturer say about each type of elephant call?
Choose your answers from the box, and write the letters A–H next to questions 38–40.

A cannot be heard by humans at all
B is usually accompanied by a leg movement
C begins and ends at the same pitch
D is usually accompanied by a nod of the head
E continuously increases in pitch
F is repeated over a long period
G continually fluctuates in volume

38. Greeting ....
39. Contact call ....
40. Summons to move on ....

To help you predict answers to Multiple Choice questions, you need to

look at the key words in the answer choices to identify:

- **Similar answers**: similar sounding words; one word differences; differences in time and tense.

- **Similar sounding words:** Usually with numbers. They sound very similar when spoken.

Examples:

1. 1930 & 1913;

2. 30,000 & 13,000

3. 1940 & 1914;

4. 40,000 & 14,000

5. 1950 & 1915;

6. 50,000 & 15,000

7. 1960 & 1916;

8. 60,000 & 16,000

9. 1970 & 1917;

10. 70,000 & 17,000

11. 1980 & 1918;

12. 80,000 & 18,000

13. 1990 & 1919;

14. 90,000 & 19,000.

- **One word differences:**

<u>Examples:</u>

1. How do most people travel to work?

     a.   Taxi

     b.   Train

     c.   *Private <u>bus</u>*

     d.   *Private <u>car</u>*

The answer will be highly likely to be **C** *(private bus)* or **D** *(private car)*

2. What kind of film does Tom like?

     a.   <u>Chinese</u> action <u>films</u>

     b.   American comedy

     c.   <u>Chinese</u> love story <u>films</u>

The answer will be highly likely to be **A** *(Chinese action films)* or **C** *(Chinese love story films)*

- **Differences in time and tense:**

When will the school be built?

A. <u>as soon as</u> they receive funding from the billionaire.

B. <u>after</u> they receive funding from the billionaire.

- **Less likely answers.**

<u>Example:</u>

What does Peter want to do in the morning?

A. go to the zoo

B. go shopping

C go to a popular nightclub

D. visit his grandparents.

We can guess that **C** might not be the answer: Tom is not likely to go to a nightclub **in the morning**. He is more likely to go to the zoo, shopping or visit his grandparents, so we should listen for these answers in the listening passage.

2.COMPLETION QUESTIONS:

In Completion questions, information is missing in one of the following:

- ## A SENTENCE

    Questions 27 – 30

    Complete the sentences below.

    Write **NO MORE THAN TWO WORDS** for each answer.

    Studying with the Open University demanded a great deal of **27** ....

    Studying and working at the same time improved Rachel's **28** .... skills.

    It was helpful that the course was structured in **29** ....

    She enjoyed meeting other students at **30** ....

- ## A FORM

Example: Form Completion

Questions 1-4

Complete the form below. Write NO MORE THAN TWO WORDS
AND/OR A NUMBER for each question.

Alpha Packers and Movers

Sales Representative Contact Details		Mark Sullivan
Customer Name		John Fernandez
Office number		1. ....
Moving from:		26 Palm Street, Sydney
	Tel:	5637 5867
Moving to:	Country:	Canada
	House/Flat:	2. ....
	Street:	3. ....
	City:	4. ....

• A TABLE

Questions 22–25

Complete the table below.

Write **NO MORE THAN TWO WORDS** for each answer.

College Facility	Information
Refectory	inform them **22** .... about special dietary requirements
23	long waiting list, apply now
Careers advice	drop-in centre for information
Fitness centre	reduced **24** .... for students
Library	includes books, journals, equipment room containing audio-visual materials
Computers	ask your **25** .... to arrange a password with the technical support team

• A FLOW CHART

Freya Stark

Born in Paris in 1893

↓

First formal education at **1** ....

↓

Worked as a **2** .... in Italy

↓

Studied at School of Oriental Studies

↓

Travelled to the Lebanon,
where she learned **3** ....

↓

Made a journey to the Syrian
mountains on a **4** ....

↓

In 1934, won a **5** .... for a book

↓

Spent a further **6** .... in the Middle East

- ## A SUMMARY PARAGRAPH

Questions 1-5

The terracotta army was made in order to 1. .... the emperor after this death in his afterlife. This funerary art has been estimated to be from the 2. .... and was discovered in 1974 by the 3. .... The majority of the sculptures were 4. .... and 5. .... sculptures of cavalry horses were also found.

Complete the summary using no more than one word and/or a number.

Buckingham Palace

Buckingham Palace is where the Queen officially resides when she is in London and is well known for its famous(1) .... which was used for the first time by a royal during an official appearance in 1851. There were (2)............ bomb hits to the palace in World War II. There are a range of services available to the royal residents in the palace which has a total of (3) .... rooms. There are 1,514 doors in the palace and 760 windows which are cleaned on a (4) .... week rotation. The Queen hosts banquets, lunches, dinners, receptions and garden parties and has over (5)..................... people visiting each year.

You need to complete the information with **words** or sometimes **a number** as your answers.

There are two prediction strategies you should use during the 30-second break to help you hear the answers to Completion questions:

- Underlining the keywords, and identifying nouns, adjectives, verbs, adverbs, prepositions and articles.

Ex: The little girl happily decided to go to the birthday party.

He	happily	decided	to	go	to	New York	to	visit	his	brother
Article	adverb	verb	To infinitive	verb	To infinitive	noun	To infinitive	verb	noun	noun

He happily decided to go to New York to visit his brother.

- Predicting possible answers from context.

3. SHORT ANSWER QUESTIONS

Short Answer questions are usually questions that begin with question words, such as:

- *What?*

- *Why?*

- *Where?*

- *When?*

- *Who?*

- *How much?*

- *How many?*

- *How often?*

These words give clues about the type of answer you should be listening for, such as *a name, an amount of money, a distance, a place, a time or a reason.*

Questions 26–30

Answer the questions below.

Write **NO MORE THAN THREE WORDS AND/OR A NUMBER** for each answer.

26   How did the students do their practical sessions?

....

27   In the second semester how often did Kira work in a hospital?

....

Answer the questions below.

Write **NO MORE THAN TWO WORDS AND/OR A NUMBER** for each answer.

26 Which books cannot be renewed by telephone or email?

....

27 How much time is allowed to return recalled books?

....

"Underwater living"

Answer the questions below.

Write **ONLY ONE WORD OR A NUMBER** from the dialogue for each answer.

1. How many days did the scientists spend under the waves?

2. What answer did Rob choose?

3. What's the name of the laboratory?

4. Where's the laboratory situated?

5. What is the world record, in minutes, for holding breath underwater?

4.LABELLING A DIAGRAM.

The diagram could be:

- **A man-made object such as a camera**

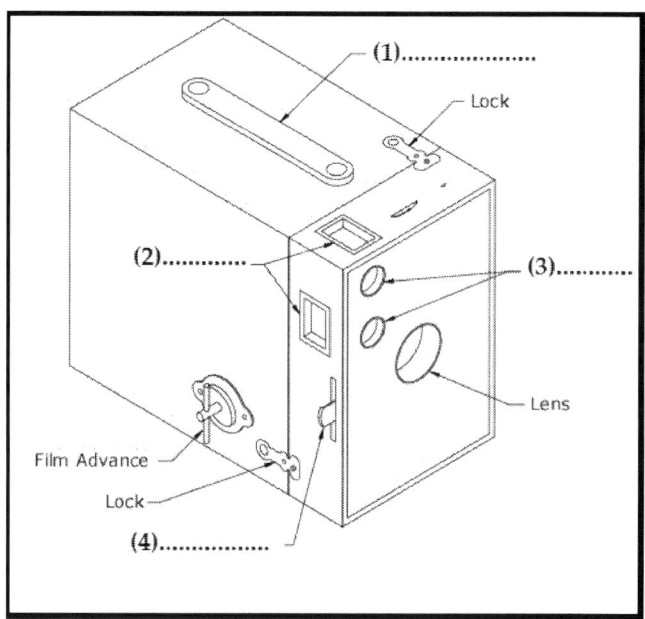

- **A natural object**

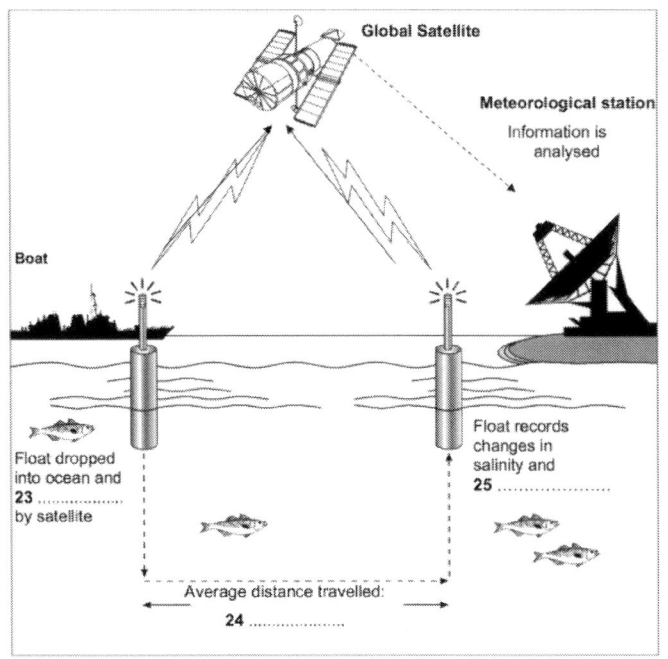

- A map of a building or a city

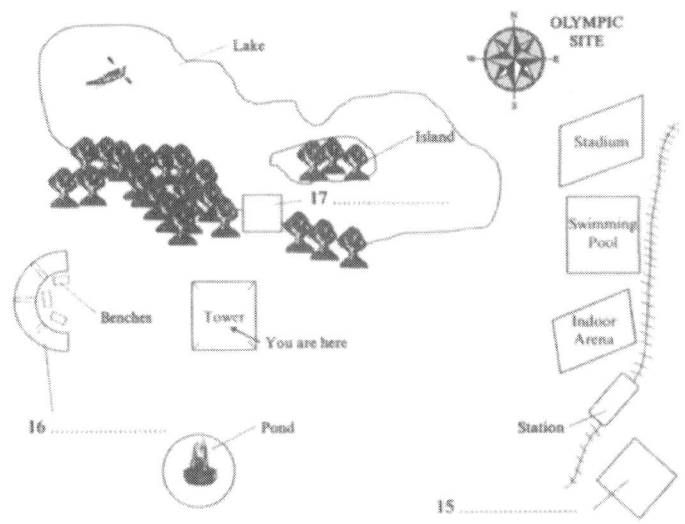

IELTS LISTENING TIPS & TRICKS

TIP 1:

Before listening:

In the IELTS test, you will have **30 seconds** at the beginning of each section to look at the Question Booklet before listening. During these 30 seconds, there are three main things you should do to improve your score:

1. Read the instructions carefully. The instructions are usually in *italics* and sometimes in **BOLD CAPITAL LETTERS**. Read the instructions carefully so that you know what to do and predict what you will hear. Think about **who** is talking, **where** they are and **what** the topic is. In the exam you will only have a short time for this, so do it as quickly as possible.

*Write **NO MORE THAN THREE WORDS** for each answer.*

Expedition Across Attora Mountains

Leader: Charles Owen

Prepared a **(11)** .... for the trip

Total length of trip **(12)** ....

Climbed highest peak in **(13)** ....

Questions 14 and 15

*Circle the correct letters **A-C**.*

14. What took the group by surprise?
    A the amount of rain
    B the number of possible routes
    C the length of the journey

15. How did Charles feel about having to change routes?
    A He reluctantly accepted it.
    B He was irritated by the diversion.
    C It made no difference to enjoyment.

If the instruction tells you to write *NO MORE THAN THREE WORDS* for each answer. This means that you are allowed to write one, two or three words as your answer. However, if you write four, or more than four words, you will receive no marks for this question, even if your answer is correct. Be careful!

If you look at your question paper, it will always tell you how many words you need for the answer. It will give you a rule. For example, if the instruction tells you to write *NO MORE THAN TWO WORDS AND/OR A NUMBER* for each answer. This means that you are allowed to write one word; you can write two words; or you can write two words and a number or you can write just a number, but you cannot write three words. Be very careful with the instructions. Make sure you pay attention to the instructions very closely.

2. Read the questions, ensure you understand them and underline the key words.

In the questions, the *key words* are usually:

Nouns: people or things *(e.g., "students", "New York", "cat", "dog", or "library")*

Verbs: actions words *(e.g., "walk", "sing", "drink", "go", or "run")*

Adjectives: words that describe nouns *(e.g., "friendly" or "beautiful", "noisy", "quiet", "big", "small")*

Adverbs: words that describe verbs *(e.g., "listen carefully" or "study hard")*

Prepositions: *e.g., "at", "in", "on", "in front of", "before", "after".*

Question words: *e.g., "who", "what". "when", "where", "why", "how", "how often", "how much", "how many", "how far", "how long", etc.*

Key words are usually **not:**

• Articles *(e.g., a, an, the)*

• Conjunctions *(e.g., and, but, or, because)*

<u>Example:</u>

<u>What subjects</u> is <u>Peter studying</u>? (The keywords are underlined)

How much does *it cost?* (The keywords are underlined)

3. Predict answer types *(e.g. name, number, noun, adjective, verb, singular, plural).*

While listening:

- Listen carefully to the instructions.

- Understand the instructions and questions.

- Only look at the key words you underlined. Do not read everything again.

- Stay focused - it's quite easy to miss the answers if you lack concentration, even for a moment.

- While you listen, write down the possible answers that you hear so that you don't forget them when you decide on the correct answer.

- Note that the answers are always in order.

After listening:

- Ensure that you have answered each question. Don't leave answers blank. Make a good guess if you are not sure.

- Check your answers and transfer them carefully to the Answer Sheet.

TIP 2:

You can write your answers in **capital letters** or **lower case**. You can choose but whatever you choose, you <u>must stay with that choice</u>. If you decide to use capital letters, all your answers must be written in capital letters. You can't change suddenly on your answer sheet. Likewise, if you choose lowercase, you must make sure that all your answers are written with lowercase on your answer sheet. Capital letters means every single letter is written as a capital. There is no difference at all; but if you're using lowercase you need to remember that some words start with a capital letter. For example, names (Mr. Johnson, Mary, Peter) or places (New York, Canada, Sydney) will start with a capital letter. Make sure if you do decide to use lowercase, you remember your capital letters at the start of your answers for **names** and **places**.

TIP 3:

Learn about the types of questions that you will get in the IELTS listening. There are quite a lot of different types of questions and you need to practice each type of question when you get in your listening test. Knowing and having a strategy, a technique for each type of question is important for your IELTS listening test. One of the most difficult types of questions is **the multiple choice**; that's often where you have A, B, or C option to choose from. However, multiple choice could also be a very long list, for example, eight options and you need to answer three questions relating to all those eight options.

There are a lot of different types of questions that you need to practice if you want to have practice with these question types then you can get a book of practice tests or you can visit online blogs where there are free practice lessons using many of these types of questions.

TIP 4:

Don't try to understand everything. The aim in IELTS for listening and reading is to find answers to questions. A correct answer is one point. All you want are **answers**. You are not aiming to understand everything. You need to look at your question, try to think of what type of answer you're looking for; listen for that answer. There will be a lot of extra information given in the recordings and you need to just relax and focus on the answers that you're looking for.

TIP 5:

You need to prepare your answers and questions quickly. Now before you listen to the recording, you will hear a message and it will say to you. You now have time to prepare **questions 1 to 5**. That means you will have time to prepare and read **questions 1, 2, 3, 4 and 5**. Then you will listen to it and after, you will have a chance to prepare question 6, 7, 8, and 9. You're always given time to prepare but it's not long. Therefore, you do need to train yourself to prepare questions quickly.

TIP 6:

Answers can come quickly, so you need to prepare for that. The answers do not come at regular intervals. You could get suddenly three answers coming together. That means you need to keep your eye on the next question. Don't just look at the question that you're looking for. Keep your eye on the other questions coming so you can move quickly to the next question and you don't lose time. You don't get lost. In addition, because the answers come quickly, you don't always have time to write long words. If the answer is *Japanese Restaurant*, you might want to just make a note. Particularly if the answer is *Japanese Restaurant*, I just note like this *"Jap res"*. You would write that on your question paper, and then when you transfer your answers to the answer sheet, you would write the full words which is *Japanese Restaurant*. Therefore, making notes is very useful. You should also make notes of possible answers because maybe you're going to miss one. You can write all over your question paper because the examiner will never see it. Make notes on your question paper, write down the short version of the word if you need to, and transfer answers correctly to your answer sheet.

TIP 7:

There may be a gap between answers. Sometimes, we have answers coming quickly, but also there could be a gap and this is when students start to panic. They're listening and waiting and waiting and there's no answer; the recording is going and going and they get very nervous. That's the reason why it's important to underline your key words because then you know that you need to wait for these words to come. Don't panic, you need to be calm and keep listening, keep your eye on the next question, make notes while you're listening and be prepared for any gaps between answers.

TIP 8:

Common traps. These are ways that IELTS really try to test your understanding and your vocabulary. Now I'll give an example of a common trap. This is when the answers are given. For example:

Shall we meet at 5 o'clock?

Yes, definitely. Let's meet at 5.

So we've got the answer *"5 o'clock"*, but then it's changed and the speaker says:

"Oh, actually sorry. How about half past seven?"

So suddenly instead of the answer *being 5*, it is now *5:30*. So when you listen and you hear your answer obviously, you can make a note of the answer but <u>keep listening</u> because <u>that answer might be changed</u>. Be careful with that. Another type of trap is when you have the same words in the question and the same words in the recording. Of course, people immediately think *"oh this is my answer"* but actually that could be **a trap** because usually IELTS will use **paraphrasing** rather than using the exact same words completely. Therefore, always be a little bit suspicious when you hear all the same words. If you want to have practice with common traps, then visit online blogs where there are lots of practice exercises with these types of traps and it will help you to practice for that.

TIP 9:

Repeated answers. This is when you've got three or four people having a discussion; and of course when they are discussing something, people might say *"is this what you mean?"*, *"Do you mean this?"* And the answer could be repeated again and that can help you to locate the answer.

TIP 10:

Listening for plural nouns. IELTS is a listening test and they know that many foreign language speakers struggle to hear plurals, so you need to pay attention to *"does that word have an "S" on the end or not?"* If you have a sentence completion, sometimes you can see in the grammar that you need a plural answer. Therefore, just take a look, but keep your ears open for those plurals.

There are three main strategies that help you improve your listening for plurals.

Strategy 1: know your uncountable nouns because they do not have the *"S"* on the end *(e.g. advice, information, equipment, milk, water, happiness, furniture).*

Strategy 2: know your vocabulary and spelling, for example, *"grass roots".* It always has an *"S"* that is how the word is written. Obviously, this is an English language test and this is testing your vocabulary.

Strategy 3: <u>be careful of linking sounds</u>. That's very important because they can make it very difficult to hear the *"S"* and if that happens, you need to use grammar to help you. If the *"S"* is not clear, think of the grammar and think about the articles. *Is there an article "a" in the question?* If there isn't, listen for the article *"a"* in the audio. Somewhere there will be an article if it's a singular.

TIP 11:

If you don't know the answer, <u>you can guess</u>. Write something on your answer sheet. Don't leave an empty space because if your answer is wrong, it will not affect your band score. You don't lose a point if your answers is wrong. Therefore, always guess if you don't know the answer.

TIP 12:

Before section 1 truly begins, you have a chance to listen to an example and see an example answer. You should use that time to <u>get used to the speaker's voices</u> because that will help you understand what they're going to say. This example is only given at the start of section 1, not at the start of section 2, 3 or 4, so use the time effectively and listen carefully to the example.

TIP 13:

Accents. The accents that come in the IELTS listening test, of course there will be a lot of British English accent and Australian accent as well. However, IELTS is an international English language test, so that means there will be a range of accents. Therefore, when you practice for your listening test, make sure you practice listening to different types of accents.

TIP 14:

Look for the title. You will often find titles on your question paper and those titles are very useful because it helps you prepare for the topic that's coming. Therefore, if you have a diagram completion, map completion, table completion questions, have a look for the Title, read it, and underline it.

TIP 15:

The technical and academic language is often not paraphrased. Not all words, but often technical and academic language are not paraphrased. If you see a very complicated word or a technical word, then that can be useful for you. Don't be scared of that language and it can be useful because it might not be paraphrased and that means when you hear it, you know what question you're on and you can keep your place.

TIP 16:

Concentration. You need to really concentrate for the IELTS listening test. If you lose focus at any time, you can not only miss an answer, but you can lose your place in the recording; and then it's very difficult to locate the following answers. Therefore, you need to practice building your concentration before you go into the real Ielts test.

Tip 17:

Pay attention to any information that answers the questions *what?, when?, where?, how?, who?, why?*

Example:

What: *an action movie.*

When: *last night.*

Where: *at the cinema.*

How: *interesting, fun.*

Who: *Jackie Chain, Bruce Willis, Dominic Purcell*

This method is very important and works in all sections of the IELTS Listening test.

Tip 18:

Because you cannot use a dictionary during the IELTS test, you have to **guess** the meaning of a word from the context of the listening passage. This is an important strategy to help you understand vocabulary while you listen.

Tip 19: identifying synonyms and rephrasing

Because the words used in the Listening test questions <u>may not be exactly the same</u> as the words you hear in the listening passages. Therefore, when you learn a new word, you need to <u>develop a wide range of vocabulary</u> by **learning synonyms** for that word.

SYNONYMS *(words that have the same or similar meaning):*

Example 1:

The original sentence "It can be difficult to choose a suitable website designer from a large number of applicants."

The paraphrased sentence "It is sometimes hard to select an appropriate website designer from many applicants."

Example 2:

The original sentence "Our car needs petrol."

The paraphrased sentence "Our vehicle requires fuel."

Example 3:

The original sentence "I enjoy reading comic books."

The paraphrased sentence "I like reading comic books."

Example 4:

The original sentence "That is a building of 15 floors."

The paraphrased sentence:

- "That is a 15-floor building."

- "That is a building which has 15 floors."

REPHRASING *(the wording of the questions is different from the wording in the listening passage):*

Example 1:

The original sentence "Tom is a very handsome actor."

The rephrased sentence "Tom is an actor who is very handsome."

Example 2:

The original sentence "Parenting can be a challenging task."

The rephrased sentence "Parenting can be a task which is challenging."

<u>Example 3:</u>

The original sentence "Watching films develops people's imagination."

The paraphrased sentence:

"People's imagination development is a positive effect of watching films."

"Film watchers can develop their imagination."

<u>Example 4:</u>

The original sentence "I gave him a watch for his birthday."

The paraphrased sentence "He was given a watch for his birthday."

<u>Tip 20</u>: distinguishing between different speakers

To do this, you need to be able to hear the difference in their voices. This particularly works when the gender of the two speakers are the same.

These are some techniques you can use to distinguish between speakers:

<u>Before you listen:</u>

1. Identify the speakers' names, underline other key words in the questions, and predict the topic of the conversation.

<u>While you listen:</u>

2. At the beginning of the conversation, listen carefully for the speakers' names.

3. Distinguish between the speakers' voices.

How do you distinguish between voices?

In order to help you to distinguish between their voices. You should pay attention to:

• **Tone:** How high or low their voice is

• **Volume:** How loudly or softly they speak

• **Accent:** A native speaker or non-native speaker accent

Tip 21: listening for time, dates, numbers, and prices.

Listening for numbers:

In the listening test, you often need to listen and write down a number, and of course, IELTS know all the problems that many students have with numbers in English and one of the common problems is the difference between 13 and 30. Even for native speakers sometimes, it can be difficult to hear the difference between 13 and 30; 15 and 50. IELTS often give you those numbers in the test to test your ability to hear and understand in English.

How did you do well this part?

Let's have a look. As you can see, we've got the *"teens (thirteen, fifteen, sixteen)"* and the *"ty (thirty, fifty, sixty)"*. Obviously, the difference is that this sound *"teens (thirteen, fifteen, sixteen)"* is much longer and this one *"ty (thirty, fifty, sixty)"* is shorter. That is the difference.

Listening for time:

In English, there is often two different ways to say the same time. Can you think of another way to say the time *2:50 (two fifty)?* Well, the other way is *ten to three*. That means *10 minutes before 3 o'clock*. So there are 2 different ways to tell the same time, and in your IELTS listening test, IELTS will often try to test you on that and trick you.

In Section 1, usually you will be asked to listen for information such as **numbers, times and dates**. These can all be expressed in different ways. For example:

1. How do you say the time **9:10**?

Answer: *nine ten or ten past nine.*

2. How do you say the time **11:20**?
Answer: *eleven twenty or twenty past eleven.*

3. How do you say the time **10:15**?

Answer: *ten fifteen/ quarter past ten.*

4. How do you say the time **2:35**?

Answer: *twenty-five to three.*

5. How do you say the time **9:45**?

Answer: *quarter to ten/ nine forty-five.*

6. How do you say the time **4:30**?

Answer: *four thirty/ half past four.*

7. How do you say the time **7:50 a.m.**?

Answer: *seven fifty a.m.*

8. How do you say the amount of money **$14.50**?

Answer: fourteen dollars and fifty cents/ fourteen dollars fifty.

9. How do you say the amount of money **$286.77**?

Answer: two hundred eighty-six dollars and seventy-seven cents.

10. How do you say the amount of money **£30.50**?

Answer: thirty pounds and fifty pence/ thirty pounds fifty.

11. How do you say the amount of money **£350.60**?

Answer: three hundred and fifty pounds and sixty pence.

12. How do you say the number **4,300**?

Answer: forty three hundred/ four thousand three hundred.

13. How do you say the number **6,500**?

Answer: six thousand five hundred/ sixty five hundred.

14. How do you say the number **3.5 million**?

Answer: three and a half million/ three point five million.

15. How do you say the number **4.45 million**?

Answer: four point four five million.

16. How do you say the number **2,350**?

Answer: two thousand three hundred and fifty/ twenty three hundred and fifty.

17. How do you say the number **4,500**?

Answer: four thousand five hundred/ forty-five hundred/ four and a half thousand

18. How do you say the number **16,500**?

Answer: sixteen and a half thousand.

19. How do you say the number **17,650**?

Answer: seventeen thousand, six hundred and fifty.

20. How do you say the number **950**?

Answer: nine hundred and forty-five.

21. How do you say the date **26 May**?

Answer: the twenty sixth of May/ May the twenty sixth.

22. How do you say the date **21 March**?

Answer: the twenty first of March/ March the twenty first.

23. How do you say the date **22/7/08**?

Answer: the twenty-second of July two thousand and eight.

24. How do you say the fraction **½**?

Answer: a half.

25. How do you say the fraction **1/3**?

Answer: one-third.

26. How do you say the fraction **¼**?

Answer: one-fourth/ one-quarter.

27. How do you say the fraction **2/3**?

Answer: two-thirds.

28. How do you say the fraction ¾?

Answer: three quarters/three fourths.

29. How do you say the telephone number **8848-5665**?

Answer: double eight four eight five double six five.

30. How do you say the telephone number **0547-447-621**?

Answer: oh five four seven double four seven six two one/ zero five four seven double four seven six two one.

31. How do you say the number **4.5%**?

Answer: four point five percent/ four and a half percent.

32. How do you say the number **6.05%**?

Answer: six point oh five percent/ six point zero five percent.

33. How do you say the number **65.80 million**?

Answer: sixty five point eighty million.

Tip 22: improving your spelling of common names and places.

Let me give you a list of strategies to help you when you listen for names.

Strategy 1: Write the capital letters. A name always starts with a capital letter. Don't forget it; don't lose a point because you forgot the capital letter.

Strategy 2: <u>Spelling</u>. If it's a long name, it will be spelt; and you need to practice your spelling to make sure that you get that name correct. Make sure you practice spelling at home.

Strategy 3: <u>Common names</u>. In the test, you will be given some names that you have to spell, and some names you don't. **Why?** Well, the reason is these names are common such as Simon, David, Mary, etc. IELTS expect you to know the spelling of common English names that means you need to learn them and practice them. So if it's a common name, IELTS probably won't spell it. However, if it is a longer name, more unusual, then they will spell it.

COMMON NAMES:

1. McDonald

2. Caroline

3. Sophia

4. Hannah

5. Allison

6. Brian

7. Bryan

8. Lawrence

9. Michael

10. Nicholas

11. Louis

12. Lauren

13. Jessica

14. Steven

15. Stephen

16. Thompson

PLACE NAMES:

1. Australia: Sydney, Melbourne, Brisbane, Canberra

2. Scotland: Edinburgh, Glasgow

3. Wales: Cardiff

4. England: London, Oxford, Cambridge

5. Ireland: Dublin, Belfast

6. Canada: Vancouver, Toronto

7. India: New Delhi, Calcutta

8. Thailand: Bangkok

9. Hungary: Budapest

10. New Zealand: Auckland, Wellington

11. The United States: Los Angeles, San Francisco, Washington D.C., New York

12. Portugal: Lisbon

13. Spain: Barcelona

14. Argentina: Buenos Aires.

15. Brazil: Sao Paolo

16. Peru: Lima

Tip 23: listening for locations and directions (map gap-fill)

COMMON LOCATION AND DIRECTION WORDS:

1. On the right of

2. To your right

3. On the left of

4. On your left

5. Next to

6. Beside

7. Ahead of you

8. In the corner

9. Near

10. Between

11. Beyond

12. Above

13. Opposite

14. In front of

15. Behind

16. Not far from

17. Across from

18. At the end of the…(hallway, street, road, etc.)

19. To the north of

20. To the south of

21. To the east of

22. To the west of

23. On the north side of

24. On the south side of

25. On the east side of

26. On the west side of

Tip 24: Listening for signposts:

How can **signposts** help you?

- Signposts will tell you at what stage you are in the listening passage (the beginning, the middle or the end).

- Signposts will help you anticipate what the speaker is going to do next.

Signpost	Function	Example
- First/ Firstly….. - Second/ Secondly….. - Third/ Thirdly….. - Final/ Finally…… - Last/ Lastly….. - Last but not least… - At the same time….. - Then….. - Meanwhile….. - As soon as….. - Since….. - After this / that….. - After….. - Before….. - While…..	Showing a sequence	*- Firstly, we learn how to clean, secondly we learn how to cook.* *- After taking five minutes to think, he finally answered that he did.* *- Last but not least, let me introduce Jessica, our new secretary.* *- After that, she went home.* *- Then, she remembered that she had once met a friend of her father's.*

- During….. - Simultaneously ….. - When….. - Following this…..		
- Due to the fact that - Due to - Because of - As a result of - Owing to	**Giving a cause**	*- The meeting was cancelled because of/ due to the bad weather.* *- As a result of the accident, Tom was out of work for three months.* *- Owing to the storm, we arrived late.* *- Due to the fact that it is raining, we cannot go hiking.*
- On the other hand.....		*- He worked hard for the test; however, he*

- However..... - On the contrary..... - But..... - Oppositely..... - Nevertheless..... - Alternatively..... - While..... - On the other hand..... - Whilst..... - Unlike..... - Even though..... - In contrast to this..... - Alternatively..... - Then again.....	**Show contrast**	*failed.* *- Although Mary was extremely tired, she washed the dishes.* *- In contrast, car prices seem to be very expensive.* *- Unlike his brother, Peter exercises every day.*
- Likewise..... - In the same way.....		*- Likewise, he is very good at French.* *- Similarly, there is no*

- Similarly.....		*rule that....*
- Similar to.....	**Show**	*- Like the previous*
- Like the previous point.....	**comparison**	*point, I think that this applies to other*
- At the same time.....		*aspects of our lives too.*
- Also.....		
- Just as.....		

- As a result..... - As an effect..... - Consequently..... - So..... - Thus..... - Therefore..... - Hence..... - The reason why..... - For this reason..... - Thereby..... - Eventually..... - Because of this	**Show consequence, effects or result**	*- Hundreds of people came to the wedding; therefore, it was not possible to say hello to everyone.* *- As a result of studying hard, he passed the exam.* *- Tom had lost his wallet, and because of this he couldn't pay for a hotel room.*
- As an example..... - For example..... - For instance..... - To show an	**Giving an example**	*- There is a similar word in many languages, for example/for instance in English and French.*

- example..... - Like..... - Namely..... - Such as..... - As..... - Particularly..... - In particular..... - As an evidence..... - To illustrate.....		- *Take the Japanese class that I took last semester as an example.* - *We would like to show an example for each condition…*
- In my opinion...... - I think..... - I strongly agree with the idea that....... - My opinion is that..... - I strongly disagree with the given topic....	**Giving Personal Opinions**	- *In my opinion, shopping is fun.* - *I think/believe he can do it.* - *I personally feel that/ From my point of view/ From my way of thinking, eating meat is unnecessary and cruel*

- In my view.....		*to animals.*
- Apparently.....		
- I believe.....		
- From my point of view.....		
- Personally speaking.....		
- To my way of thinking.....		
- It seems to me that.....		
- To me.....		
- I feel that.....		
- It appears that.....		
- I suppose.....		
- What do you think about...?	**Asking for Opinions**	*- What do you think about White Smoke?*
- How do you feel about ...?		*- How do you feel about the issue?*
- What are your		*- What are your views*

- views on....? - Don't you think...?		*on climate change?* *- Don't you think she did a great job?*
- Yes. - You're right. - I suppose you're right. - I think you're right. - I believe you're right. - Exactly. - Definitely. - Absolutely. - I completely agree that..... - I strongly agree..... - I quite agree that.... - I agree with the	**Agreeing**	*- I couldn't agree more. We've got to do something.* *- I completely agree that this is the best way to tackle the issue.*

opinion that.....		
- I totally agree with the given idea that.....		
- I could not agree more.....		
- I am quite inclined to the opinion that.....		
- I concur with the group who believe that.....		
- I accept the fact that.....		
- I accept that.....		
- I am in agreement.....		
- I approve the idea.....		
- I consent that.....		
- Yes, but..... - (I'm afraid) I don't (really)		- *I don't really agree with you.* - *I (completely)*

agree.		*disagree with you.*
- I can't say that I agree.	**Disagreeing**	*- I can't say that I agree with your point on…..*
- I (completely) disagree.		*- I wouldn't say that he is honest.*
- I don't think so.		
- I doubt it.		
- I wouldn't say that.		
- Not really.		
- I strongly disagree…..		
- I disagree with the opinion that….		
- I completely disagree with…..		
- I disagree with the statement…..		
- I totally disagree with the given idea		

that.....		
- I disagree with the group of people.....		
- I quite oppose the opinion that.....		
- I totally do not accept the fact that.....		
- I disapprove that.....		
- My own opinion contradicts.....		
- However, my opinion is different.....		
- Provided that..... - Providing that..... - If..... - Unless..... - For this reason.....	**Expressing condition**	*- She will come provided that she is well enough.* *- Providing that the weather is fine, we'll have a picnic on Sunday.* *- If you don't hurry,*

- Because of that….. - In case….. - So that…..		*you will be late for the movie.* - *Unless you hurry, we will be late for the movie.*
- Definitely….. - Certainly….. - Of course….. - No doubt….. - Without any doubt….. - Doubtlessly….. - Undoubtedly…..	**Expressing certainty**	- *He will definitely/certainly be at the airport to meet you.* - *Without any doubt/ Undoubtedly, he is guilty.*
- Furthermore….. - In addition….. - Moreover….. - And….. - As well as…..	**Adding further information**	- *Furthermore/ In addition, purchase of new equipment will help cut manufacturing costs.* - *He is clever, and*

- Also….. - Besides….. - What's more…..		*moreover, he is handsome.* *- Besides, I enjoy living alone.*
- In conclusion….. - To conclude….. - In summary….. - On the whole….. - To sum up….. - To conclude with….. - To summarize….. - All in all, - In short….. - Overall…..	**To show the conclusion part**	*- To sum up, there are three main ways of ...* *- In conclusion/ In summary/ All in all, some people are better suited to working from home than others.* *- To sum up/ To conclude/ In short, some improvements in the middle school program need to be made.*

Tip 25: Listening for stressed words

In the IELTS Listening test, when speakers want to give facts or express their opinions, they usually use stress to emphasise their important words. Therefore, recognizing stress will help you hear an answer related to both facts and speakers' opinions.

Tip 26: Practice

In order to prepare and practice for the IELTS listening test, you should:

1. Go through and practice listening as many tests in the official Cambridge IELTS books as possible.

2. Improve your listening skill by doing as many listening test samples as possible on the official IELTS website https://www.ielts.org/about-the-test/sample-test-questions

3. Analyze your mistakes when you finish listening a test.

4. For difficult parts of each test, try to listen to them several times until you understand all of the correct answers.

5. Write down and learn new vocabulary that are presented in each test.

ONLINE DICTIONARIES

Oxford Learner's Dictionary

https://www.oxfordlearnersdictionaries.com/

Cambridge Dictionary

http://dictionary.Cambridge.org

Longman Dictionary

https://www.ldoceonline.com/

Merriam-Webster Dictionary

http://www.meriam-webster.com

THE ANSWER SHEET:

You can see that there are spaces for **40 answers**. You have **10 minutes** at the end of the test to transfer your answers from your Question Booklet to the Answer Sheet. It's very important for you to practice using it before you go into your IELTS test.

IELTS Listening and Reading Answer Sheet

Centre number:

Pencil must be used to complete this sheet.

Please write your full name in CAPITAL letters on the line below.

Then write your six digit Candidate number in the boxes and shade the number in the grid on the right.

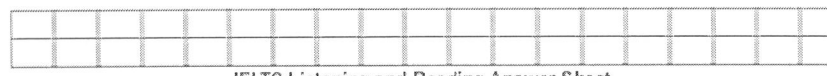

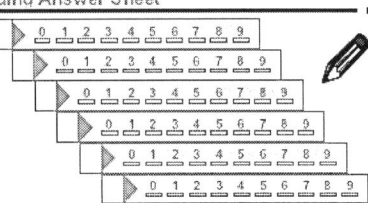

0 1 2 3 4 5 6 7 8 9
0 1 2 3 4 5 6 7 8 9
0 1 2 3 4 5 6 7 8 9
0 1 2 3 4 5 6 7 8 9
0 1 2 3 4 5 6 7 8 9
0 1 2 3 4 5 6 7 8 9

Test date (shade ONE box for the day, ONE box for the month and ONE box for the year):

Day: 01 02 03 04 05 06 07 08 09 10 11 12 13 14 15 16 17 18 19 20 21 22 23 24 25 26 27 28 29 30 31

Month: 01 02 03 04 05 06 07 08 09 10 11 12 **Year** (last 2 digits): 09 10 11 12 13 14 15 16 17 18

	Listening Listening Listening Listening Listening Listening	Marker use only			Marker use only
1		✓ 1 ✗	21		✓ 21 ✗
2		✓ 2 ✗	22		✓ 22 ✗
3		✓ 3 ✗	23		✓ 23 ✗
4		✓ 4 ✗	24		✓ 24 ✗
5		✓ 5 ✗	25		✓ 25 ✗
6		✓ 6 ✗	26		✓ 26 ✗
7		✓ 7 ✗	27		✓ 27 ✗
8		✓ 8 ✗	28		✓ 28 ✗
9		✓ 9 ✗	29		✓ 29 ✗
10		✓ 10 ✗	30		✓ 30 ✗
11		✓ 11 ✗	31		✓ 31 ✗
12		✓ 12 ✗	32		✓ 32 ✗
13		✓ 13 ✗	33		✓ 33 ✗
14		✓ 14 ✗	34		✓ 34 ✗
15		✓ 15 ✗	35		✓ 35 ✗
16		✓ 16 ✗	36		✓ 36 ✗
17		✓ 17 ✗	37		✓ 37 ✗
18		✓ 18 ✗	38		✓ 38 ✗
19		✓ 19 ✗	39		✓ 39 ✗
20		✓ 20 ✗	40		✓ 40 ✗

Note: don't ever leave your answers blank, or they will be marked incorrect. If you cannot find the right answer, you can guess.

LISTENING STRATEGIES

Listening for relaxation

Listening for relaxation is important since you can choose to listen to what you are interested in. For example:

- Short stories
- Songs
- Movies

While you are listening for relaxation, you <u>don't need to take notes</u>. If you want to know the meaning of a new word, <u>write it down immediately</u> while you are listening and <u>then use your dictionary to find the meaning later</u>. This way helps you be able to keep relaxing without worrying that you must understand and learn every new word you hear.

Listening for main ideas

This method helps you **listen for general information** rather than specific details. For example, you could listen for things such as:

- The general topic
- Cause and effect
- Problems and solutions
- Comparisons and contrasts

Listening for main ideas will help you understand and follow the context of a conversation. This way then help you to **identify the specific information for your answers** in the test.

Listening for specific information

This means you need to focus on listening for details such as:

- **Numbers:** *dates, times, amounts, percentages, credit card details, telephone numbers, etc.*
- **Names:** *places (eg, names of streets, countries, cities), people, groups and organisations, etc.*

Listening again and again

I recommend that you should listen to the same recording several times when you practice listening to anything in English at home. This way will help you learn or find something new when you listen again and certainly improve your listening skill more quickly than if you only listened to everything once.

CONCLUSION

Thank you again for downloading this book on *"IELTS Listening Strategies: The Ultimate Guide With Tips, Tricks, And Practice On How To Get A Target Band Score Of 8.0+ In 10 Minutes A Day."* and reading all the way to the end. I'm extremely grateful.

If you know of anyone else who may benefit from the useful strategies, structures, tips, guides for IELTS listening that are revealed in this book, please help me inform them of this book. I would greatly appreciate it.

Finally, if you enjoyed this book and feel that it has added value to your work and study in any way, please take a couple of minutes to share your thoughts and post a REVIEW on Amazon. Your feedback will help me to continue to write other books of IELTS topic that helps you get the best results. Furthermore, if you write a simple REVIEW with positive words for this book on Amazon, you can help hundreds or perhaps thousands of other readers who may want to improve their English Listening skill sounding like a native speaker. Like you, they worked hard for every penny they spend on books. With the information and recommendation you provide, they would be more likely to take action right away. We really look forward to reading your review.

Thanks again for your support and good luck!

If you enjoy my book, please write a POSITIVE REVIEW on Amazon.

-- Rachel Mitchell --

CHECK OUT OTHER BOOKS

Go here to check out other related books that might interest you:

Ielts Writing Task 2 Samples : Over 450 High-Quality Model Essays for Your Reference to Gain a High Band Score 8.0+ In 1 Week (Box set) https://www.amazon.com/dp/B077BYQLPG

Ielts Academic Writing Task 1 Samples: Over 450 High Quality
Samples for Your Reference to Gain a High Band Score 8.0+ In 1
Week (Box set) https://www.amazon.com/dp/B077CC5ZG4

Shortcut To English Collocations: Master 2000+ English Collocations
In Used Explained Under 20 Minutes A Day (5 books in 1 Box set)

https://www.amazon.com/dp/B06W2P6S22

IELTS Writing Task 1 + 2: The Ultimate Guide with Practice to Get a
Target Band Score of 8.0+ In 10 Minutes a Day

https://www.amazon.com/dp/B075DFYPG6

IELTS Speaking Strategies: The Ultimate Guide With Tips, Tricks, And Practice On How To Get A Target Band Score Of 8.0+ In 10 Minutes A Day.

https://www.amazon.com/dp/B075JCW65G

Shortcut To Ielts Writing: The Ultimate Guide To Immediately Increase Your Ielts Writing Scores.

https://www.amazon.com/dp/B01JV7EQGG

Common English Mistakes Explained With Examples: Over 600 Mistakes Almost Students Make and How to Avoid Them in Less Than 5 Minutes A Day

https://www.amazon.com/dp/B072PXVHNZ

Paraphrasing Strategies: 10 Simple Techniques For Effective Paraphrasing In 5 Minutes Or Less

https://www.amazon.com/dp/B071DFG27Q

Legal Vocabulary In Use: Master 600+ Essential Legal Terms And
Phrases Explained In 10 Minutes A Day

http://www.amazon.com/dp/B01L0FKXPU

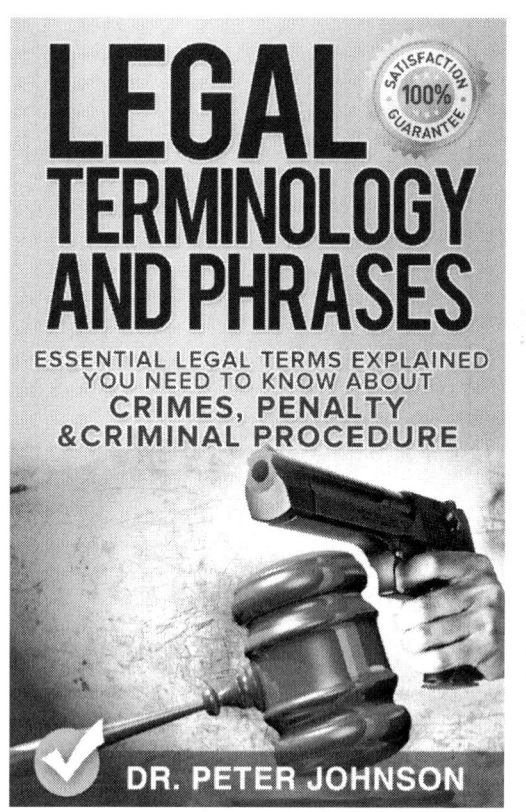

Legal Terminology And Phrases: Essential Legal Terms Explained
You Need To Know About Crimes, Penalty And Criminal Procedure

http://www.amazon.com/dp/B01L5EB54Y

Productivity Secrets For Students: The Ultimate Guide To Improve Your Mental Concentration, Kill Procrastination, Boost Memory And Maximize Productivity In Study

http://www.amazon.com/dp/B01JS52UT6

Daughter of Strife: 7 Techniques On How To Win Back Your Stubborn Teenage Daughter

https://www.amazon.com/dp/B01HS5E3V6

Parenting Teens With Love And Logic: A Survival Guide To
Overcoming The Barriers Of Adolescence About Dating, Sex And
Substance Abuse

https://www.amazon.com/dp/B01JQUTNPM

http://www.amazon.com/dp/B01K0ARNA4

Printed in Great Britain
by Amazon